REPUBLIC XF-84H "THUNDERSCREECH" TU

Above, the number one XF-84H, S/N 51-17059, on its maiden flight on 22 July 1955 with Republic test pilot Henry G. Beaird at the controls. Note Beaird's Confederate flag in the aft canopy window. (USAF)

INTRODUCTION: In 1951, engineers at the Air Force's Propeller Laboratory at Wright-Patterson AFB, Dayton, OH, wanted a test bed for supersonic propellers in order to continue the work that had been done on their XP-81 "Silver Bullet" escort fighter and the Navy's XF2R-1 "Darkshark" carrier fighter. Both these aircraft were powered by a small GE TG-100 turboprop engine in the nose and a turbojet engine in the tail. The XP-81 had a GE I-40 (J33) and the XF2R-1 had a GE I-16 turbojet engine. Although both planes had a tremendous rate-of-climb for the period (1946-1947), their overall performance offered too little improvement over current frontline aircraft.

On paper, turboprop aircraft offered distinct advantages over the early jets in service. The major advantage was instant acceleration. Pure jets accelerated so poorly that a large number of pilots ended their lives when they got too low-and-slow on final and could not accelerate to safety when power was added. The jet's slow acceleration also dictated excessive take-off runs and much longer runways. In many instances, combat loads were compromised due to take-off distances required. Torque rolls while landing propeller fighters which had ended many novice P/F-51 pilots lives were resolved with a turboprop which ran at a constant propeller rpm. So the Propeller Laboratory wanted see if it could harness the speed of the jet and the responsiveness of a constant speed propeller that a turbojet offered.

The Air Force contacted with Republic Aviation to build two supersonic propeller test vehicles. Republic had made its name with the supuerlative WWII P-47 "Thunderbolt" and was producing one of the three jet fighters in use in Korea, the F-84G "Thunderjet". The Thunderjet had been re-invented into a swept-winged fighter as the F-84F and then into a swept-winged photo bird, the RF-84F. The photo nose on the RF-84F caused the jet's intake to be moved from the nose to the wing roots which left the nose free to receive a turboprop engine. The new aircraft would be designated the XF-106 at first before becoming the XF-84H. Initially, a six-blade, contra-rotating propeller was planned, but was discarded in favor of assorted three and four blade single propeller designs. Three propeller manufacturers were contracted to provide test propellers: Aeroproducts, Curtiss, and Hamilton Standard.

The potential benefits of such aircraft for naval operations was even more attractive to the US Navy than to the USAF. Because of this, the Navy showed enough interest in the program that a third aircraft was planned to be built for the Navy. However, during production the Navy pulled out and the third aircraft was not produced.

The engine chosen for the XF-84H was an afterburning variation of the Allison T40, the XT40-A-1. Even though the Navy pulled out of the XF-84H program, it would incorporate the T40 into five different aircraft contacts: one transport, one single-engine carrier attack plane, one twin-engine heavy attack plane, and two destroyer based vertical take-off fighters. Only the twelve four-engine flying boats, the Convair R3Y-1/2 "Tradewinds", saw limited success with VR-2 from 1956-1958. It used non-afterburning T40-A-10 engines.

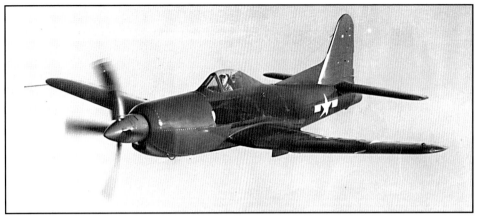

The attack aircraft was the Douglas A2D-1 "Skyshark", which flew with XT40-A-2 engines of 5,100lbs shp. The 1st of two prototypes flew in 1950 and the 1st of ten production A2D-2s flew in 1953. After much test work with Douglas and Allison, the aircraft were retired in 1955. The heavy attack aircraft was the North American XA2J-1 "Super Savage" that first flew in 1952 with two T40-A-6 engines. Two aircraft were built, but the second never flew as the XA2J-1s performance was inferior to that of the AJ-1/2. The two VTOL fighters, the Convair XFY-1 "Pogo" and the Lockheed XFV-1 both used YT40-A-14 engines. Both aircraft were operated in 1954-1955 with only the Convair XFY-1 receiving the vertical rated engine. The Lockheed XFV-1 was fitted with a spindley temporary landing gear for flight testing and never took off vertically like the Pogo did. When the flight test program ended, Hiller received the XFV-1 and its spare engine for use in its T-40 test pro-

---

At left, top-to-bottom: The 1947 Ryan XF2R-1 "DarkShark" (see Naval Fighters #28) was a composite turboprop and jet engine development of the FR-1 "Fireball" which utilized a Wright Cyclone R-1820-72W 1,350hp radial engine and a GE I-16 1,600lb thrust turbojet. The prop engine in FR-1, BuNo 39661, was replaced with a GE TG-100 turboprop to produce this truely attractive aircraft. (RYAN) The military's first turboprop aircraft was the Convair XP-81 (see Air Force Legends # 214) that was powered by a GE TG-100 turboprop and a GE I-40 (J33) turbojet. First flight of the XP-81, S/N 44-91000, with a TG-100 in the nose was on 21 December 1945. It is seen here on 25 January 1946 with chief test pilot Sam Shannon at the controls. (Convair) The four engine Convair R3Y Tradewind (see Naval Fighters #34) was powered by Allison T40 turboprop engines. This R3Y-2 was one of six built. Six R3Y-1s preceded these as did one XP5Y-1. (Convair) Douglas XA2D-1, BuNo 122988, seen here in flight showed real promise until the unreliability of the T40 caused its demise as it did with all other T40 aircraft projects. The "Skyshark" utilized the T40-A-2 engine. (Harry Gann)

grams. By 1956, Hiller received a contract to build the tilt-wing X-18. It was powered by two of the XT40-A-14s mounted on the tilt-wing and a Westinghouse J34 mounted in the tail to power the tail mounted pitch controls. It was flown until 1962, when it was grounded, but continued to be used in the VTOL Ground Effect Simulation Program at Edwards AFB into 1964. During its flight test program, the T40-A-14 engines were kept running from parts received from the Navy's retired Tradewind fleet.

All of these T40 powered aircraft used six-blade contra-rotating propellers with each three blades of opposite rotation being powered by its own engine and drive shaft. In the XF-84H, the power of the two engines was harnessed to drive the single Aeroproducts three-blade propeller.

At top right, the 1952 North American XA2J-1 "Super Savage" used T40-A-6 engines. (USN) Above, the Hiller X-18 received the surplus YT40-A-14s from the XFV-1 when its program was terminated. (DOD) Below left, the Convair XFY-1 "Pogo" landing on 28 January 1955 used the only vertical YT40-A-14. (USN) Below right, Lockheed XFV-1 also powered by the YT40-A-14. (USN)

REPUBLIC XF-84H LEADING PARTICULARS

GENERAL:

SPAN	33ft 6.2in
LENGTH	51ft 4.2in
HEIGHT	15ft 4.7in
PROP CLEARANCE	11in
PROP DIAMETER	12ft 0.0in
DESIGN GROSS WEIGHT	22,552lbs
COMBAT WEIGHT	24,217lbs
MAX GROSS WEIGHT	29,252lbs
LANDING WEIGHT	18,993lbs

WINGS:

AIRFOIL SECTION	NACA 64, A010
WING LOADING	91.3lbs/sq ft
CHORD at ROOT	12ft 4.0in
CHORD at TIP	07ft 2.0in
INCIDENCE at ROOT	2.5°
INCIDENCE at TIP	2.5°
CATHEDRAL	3.5°
SWEEPBACK (25% chord line)	40°

STABILATOR:

SPAN	14ft 2.0in
CHORD	04ft 0.0in
INCIDENCE	0°
CATHEDRAL	0°
DIHEDRAL	0°
SWEPTBACK	40°

FUSELAGE:

MAX WIDTH	04ft 4.0in
MAX HEIGHT	07ft 3.3in
LENGTH	46ft 7.3in

AREAS:

WINGS	325sq ft
AILERONS	27.5sq ft
FLAPS	30.5sq ft
SLATS	22.8sq ft
STABILATOR	55.8sq ft
FIN	45.3sq ft
RUDDER	15.7sq ft

RANGE OF MOVEMENT:

AILERONS, UP or DOWN	18°
STABILATOR, UP	6°
STABILATOR, DOWN	15°
RUDDER, RIGHT	35°
RUDDER, LEFT	15°
AILERON TRIM, UP or Down	9°
STABILATOR TRIM, UP	3°
STABILATOR TRIM, DOWN	7°
RUDDER TRIM, RIGHT	20°
RUDDER TRIM, LEFT	6°
FLAPS, CLOSED (3-position)	0°
FLAPS, DROOP	20°
FLAPS, DOWN	40°
FLAPERON, UP or DOWN (at 0° flap)	10°
FLAPERON, UP or DOWN (20° flap)	10°
FLAPERON, UP or DOWN (40° flap)	10°
TAKE-OFF FIN, RIGHT	10°
SPEED BRAKES	60°

MAIN GEAR:

TREAD	20ft 2.31in
SHOCK STRUTS, Cleveland Pneumatic No. 9231 L/R	
WHEELS, 32x6.6in GOODYEAR No. PD-466	
TIRES, 32x6.6in GOODYEAR TYPE VII, 14-ply	
BRAKES, 32x6.6in GOODYEAR No. PD-466, Hydraulic	

NOSE GEAR:

SHOCK STRUT, Cleveland Pneumatic No. 9230A
WHEEL, 24x5.5in GOODYEAR TYPE VII
TIRE, 24x5.5in GOODYEAR TYPE VII, 12-ply
STEERING DAMPER, Houdaille-Hershey No. A-17262

TURBOPROP ENGINE:

ALLISON XT-40-A-1, Model 500B-2, Spec. No. 349A

ENGINE RPM	14,300 RPM
SHAFT HORSE POWER	5,332 SHP
JET THRUST	1,296lbs

PROPELLER:

Aeroproducts No. A39SFN-125, Supersonic, 12ft dia

BLADE DESIGN No.	D91A1-144-0
ALTERNATE PROP, Curtiss-Wright	C848S-A2
ALT. PROP, Hamilton Standard B46P4-7/6P11A3-6	

FUEL and OIL:

FUSELAGE TANK (5)	617gal
INTERNAL WING FUEL CELLS (9)	183gal
DROPPABLE WING TANKS (2)	230gal (each)
WING DROP TANKS, optional (2)	450gal (each)
OIL TANK (1)	10gal

HYDRAULIC FLUID, Mil Spec MIL-O-5606

MAIN TANK (1)	3.86gal
EMERGENCY TANK (1)	.476gal

PERFORMANCE:

MAX SPEED at SEA LEVEL	680mph
MAX SPEED at 36,000ft	639mph
COMBAT SPEED	523mph
AVERAGE CRUISE SPEED	396mph
CRUISE SPEED at 36,000ft	456mph
MAX RATE of CLIMB	5,230ft/min
COMBAT CEILING	39,800ft
SERVICE CEILING	25,250ft
COMBAT RADIUS	892 miles
FERRY RANGE	2,356 miles
STALL SPEED (power off)	143kn
TAKE-OFF DISTANCE at SEA LEVEL	6,180ft
TAKE-OFF to CLEAR 50ft	8,610ft
LANDING ROLL at SEA LEVEL	3,055ft

XF-84H GENERAL DESCRIPTION

The experimental, supersonic propeller XF-84H afterburning turboprop aircraft, based on the Republic RF-84F, was an all-metal, swept-back mid-wing, single place fighter-type airplane. It had a swept-back T-tail with a one-piece, maneuverable horizontal stabilizer mounted at the top of the rudder. The plastic fin tip contained the AN/ARC-33 radio antenna in its nose.

A movable, two-position small triangular dorsal fin ("take-off fin", or "votex gate") was located just aft of the canopy to partially overcome the effects of the propeller torque during low speed, high torque conditions (take-off and landing). The two-position fin had a maximum deflection of 10° and was controlled by a switch in the pilot's compartment.

The XF-84H was the first US aircraft to be built with a "RAT" (Ram Air Turbine), which pin-wheeled when deployed in the airstream and provided electrical and hydraulic power. The XF-84H had a voracious appetite for both, and with the landing gear deployed its needs were greater than the aircraft's ability to provide so the RAT automatically deployed when the engine was on and the gear was down. It worked so well that all tactical aircraft that followed the "Thunderscreech" were equipped with RATs for emergency purposes. The RAT was located on the right aft upper fuselage and dorsal fin.

The semi-monocoque fuselage was constructed of aluminum alloy circular/elliptical sections built up of bulkheads/beltframes and joined with extruded longerons. This was covered with fully stressed stamped and flush riveted skins. It was built in two sections separable at station 367.625 to access the power plant. The engine inlets were in the winglets adjacent to the fuselage and the afterburner was in the aft fuselage.

The cockpit was covered by a hinged (up-and-aft), manually operated canopy, which was equipped with an explosive-pneumatic system for emergency jettisoning and the ejection seat was made by Weber. The cockpit was pressurized to 5 psi and was heated or cooled by high pressure air bled from the engine compressor. The cockpit temperature was regulated by mixing hot air with air cooled by an intercooler-turbine system.

The utility system included a high-pressure demand oxygen system, fire and overheat warning systems, anti-g suit provisions, and defrosting and anti-fogging systems for the transparent panels in the cabin.

XF-84H AIRCRAFT DIMENSIONS

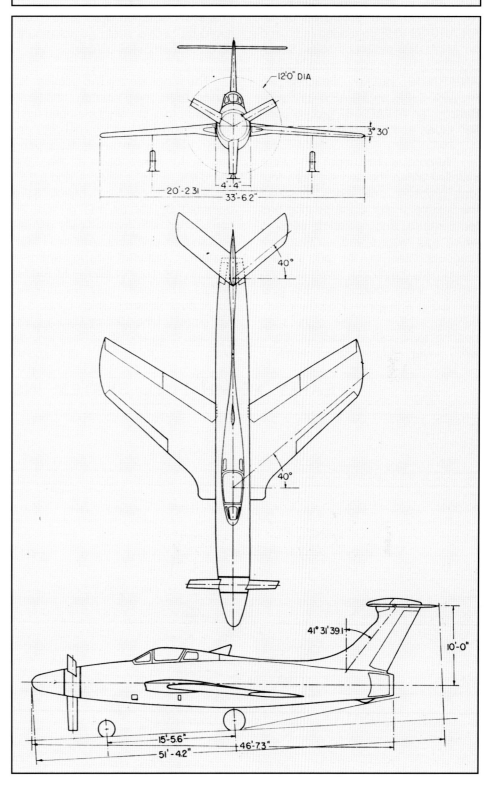

Normal electronics were minimal due the aircraft's mission as a research ship. It consisted of an AN/ARC-33 VHF command radio and an AN/ARN-6 radio compass. Space provisions were also made for an AN/ARN-12 marker beacon, an AN/APX-6 IFF, an AN/APW-11 Radar Beacon, an AN/APN-82 ground position radar, and an automatic pilot.

Numerous bearings (8) were installed along the two eighteen foot long propeller driveshafts to stiffen the flexible shafts. Each bearing had temperature and vibration sensors which had meters and warning light readouts fitted on the pilot's glare shield. An additional five vibration sensors were located on the gear box, along with six on the power section. In addition to the eight shaft bearing temperature readings, there were eleven aft fuselage critical frame temperature sensors and an ice bottle temperature reference reading. Propeller vibration was also monitered by twelve strain gages mounted on one propeller blade.

The wings were a two-section, full cantilevered multi-sparred unit covered with fully stressed stamped flush rivetted skin that had internal corrugations in high stress areas. Each wing had a 40° sweepback at the 25% chord line, a 3.5° cathedral and a 2.5° incidence. The surface controls were operated by cables and or rods in conjunction with hydraulically actuated tandem cylinders. Artificial "feel" systems induced representative loads in the control stick and rudder pedals. The loads may be trimmed out through controls which cause displacement of the surface controls feel devices. Drag and lift devices include wing slats, flaperons, and speed brakes installed at the extreme end of the aft fuselage between stations 519 and 553.

The hydraulic system operated the landing gear, slats, flaperons, speed brakes, surface control actuator, and main wheel brakes. In an emergency, the RAT would operate the hydraulic surface control actuator and a pneumatic system would operate the landing gear under emergency conditions.

The tricycle landing gear consisted of two main gears which retracted inboard into the wings, and a steerable nose gear which retracted aft into the fuselage. When retracted, each gear was enclosed by flush type doors. A combination steering device and shimmy damper was installed on the nose gear along with a mud guard.

EARLY XF-84H FUEL SYSTEM INSTALLATION

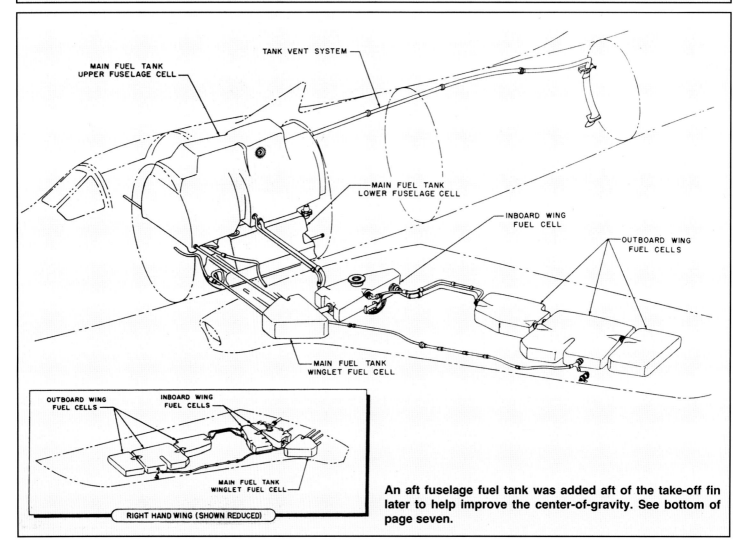

An aft fuselage fuel tank was added aft of the take-off fin later to help improve the center-of-gravity. See bottom of page seven.

FUEL TANK LOCATION and QUANTITIES

WING TANK LOCATION

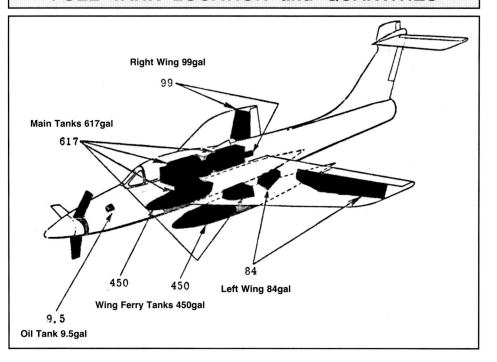

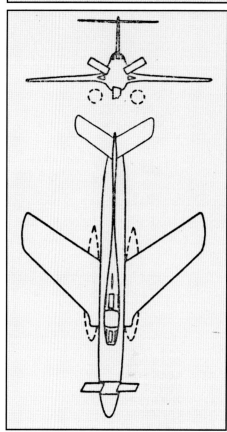

In addition to the space and weight provisions for electronics, the XF-84H was completed with space and weight provisions for a T-45 .60cal, 1,200 round gatling-gun in the nose; twenty-eight 5" HVARs on the wings; and provisions for up to 4,000lbs of bombs on two wing pylons. These provisions were designed into the XF-84H in the hope that the experimental turboprop would have sufficient performance to be developed into a viable combat plane.

Above, although never fitted, provisions were made to mate 230 or 450gal wing tanks in the locations above.

XF-84H SERVICING DATA CUTAWAY

1.) MAIN HYDRAULIC RESERVOIR, 3.86gal
2.) MAIN HYDRAULIC RESERVOIR FILLER was accessible through door 194 on the right side of the fuselage.
3.) OXYGEN BOTTLES (3), 1,800 to 1,850 psi
4.) PNEUMATIC BOTTLE FILLER
5.) PNEUMATIC BOTTLE, 3,000 psi
6.) SINGLE POINT FUEL FILLER
7.) FUEL TANK
8.) MAIN WHEELS
9.) AIR CONDITIONING UNIT
10.) PNEUMATIC STARTER
11.) OXYGEN BOTTLE FILLER
12.) BATTERY
13.) OIL TANK, 9.5gal
14.) OIL TANK FILLER

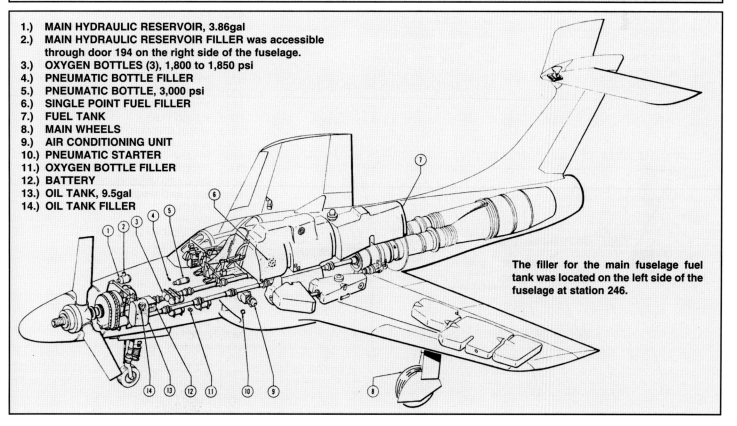

The filler for the main fuselage fuel tank was located on the left side of the fuselage at station 246.

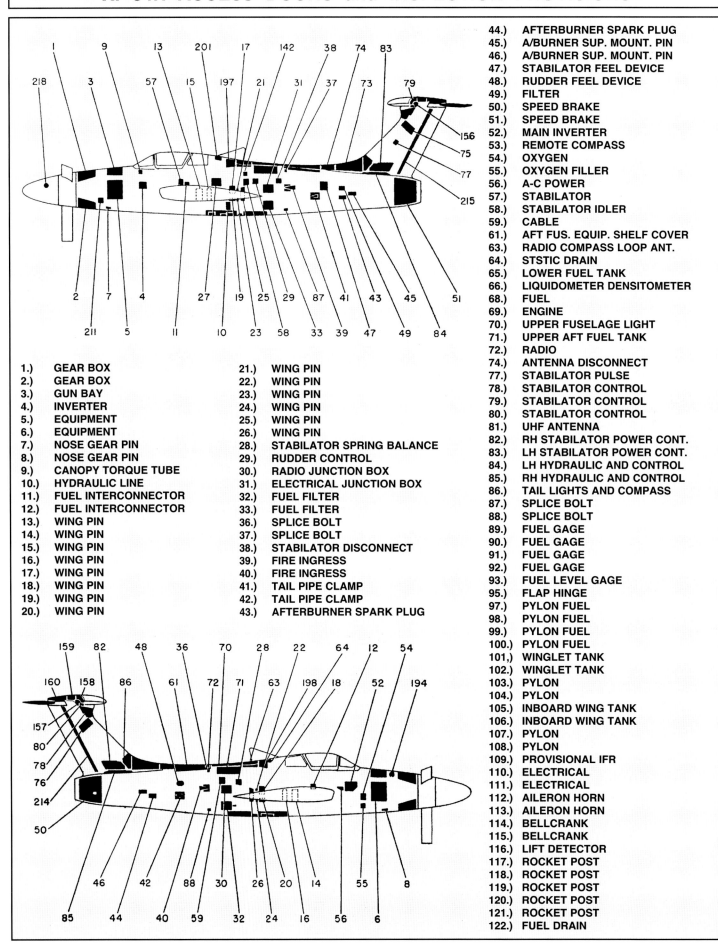

XF-84H ACCESS DOORS and INSPECTION PROVISIONS

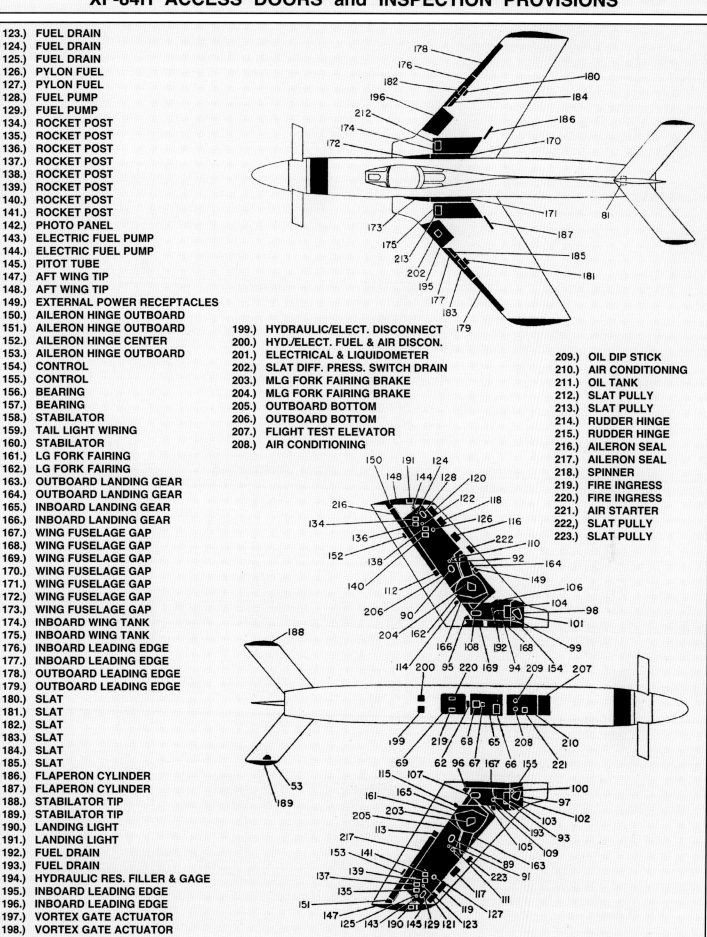

- 123.) FUEL DRAIN
- 124.) FUEL DRAIN
- 125.) FUEL DRAIN
- 126.) PYLON FUEL
- 127.) PYLON FUEL
- 128.) FUEL PUMP
- 129.) FUEL PUMP
- 134.) ROCKET POST
- 135.) ROCKET POST
- 136.) ROCKET POST
- 137.) ROCKET POST
- 138.) ROCKET POST
- 139.) ROCKET POST
- 140.) ROCKET POST
- 141.) ROCKET POST
- 142.) PHOTO PANEL
- 143.) ELECTRIC FUEL PUMP
- 144.) ELECTRIC FUEL PUMP
- 145.) PITOT TUBE
- 147.) AFT WING TIP
- 148.) AFT WING TIP
- 149.) EXTERNAL POWER RECEPTACLES
- 150.) AILERON HINGE OUTBOARD
- 151.) AILERON HINGE OUTBOARD
- 152.) AILERON HINGE CENTER
- 153.) AILERON HINGE OUTBOARD
- 154.) CONTROL
- 155.) CONTROL
- 156.) BEARING
- 157.) BEARING
- 158.) STABILATOR
- 159.) TAIL LIGHT WIRING
- 160.) STABILATOR
- 161.) LG FORK FAIRING
- 162.) LG FORK FAIRING
- 163.) OUTBOARD LANDING GEAR
- 164.) OUTBOARD LANDING GEAR
- 165.) INBOARD LANDING GEAR
- 166.) INBOARD LANDING GEAR
- 167.) WING FUSELAGE GAP
- 168.) WING FUSELAGE GAP
- 169.) WING FUSELAGE GAP
- 170.) WING FUSELAGE GAP
- 171.) WING FUSELAGE GAP
- 172.) WING FUSELAGE GAP
- 173.) WING FUSELAGE GAP
- 174.) INBOARD WING TANK
- 175.) INBOARD WING TANK
- 176.) INBOARD LEADING EDGE
- 177.) INBOARD LEADING EDGE
- 178.) OUTBOARD LEADING EDGE
- 179.) OUTBOARD LEADING EDGE
- 180.) SLAT
- 181.) SLAT
- 182.) SLAT
- 183.) SLAT
- 184.) SLAT
- 185.) SLAT
- 186.) FLAPERON CYLINDER
- 187.) FLAPERON CYLINDER
- 188.) STABILATOR TIP
- 189.) STABILATOR TIP
- 190.) LANDING LIGHT
- 191.) LANDING LIGHT
- 192.) FUEL DRAIN
- 193.) FUEL DRAIN
- 194.) HYDRAULIC RES. FILLER & GAGE
- 195.) INBOARD LEADING EDGE
- 196.) INBOARD LEADING EDGE
- 197.) VORTEX GATE ACTUATOR
- 198.) VORTEX GATE ACTUATOR
- 199.) HYDRAULIC/ELECT. DISCONNECT
- 200.) HYD./ELECT. FUEL & AIR DISCON.
- 201.) ELECTRICAL & LIQUIDOMETER
- 202.) SLAT DIFF. PRESS. SWITCH DRAIN
- 203.) MLG FORK FAIRING BRAKE
- 204.) MLG FORK FAIRING BRAKE
- 205.) OUTBOARD BOTTOM
- 206.) OUTBOARD BOTTOM
- 207.) FLIGHT TEST ELEVATOR
- 208.) AIR CONDITIONING
- 209.) OIL DIP STICK
- 210.) AIR CONDITIONING
- 211.) OIL TANK
- 212.) SLAT PULLY
- 213.) SLAT PULLY
- 214.) RUDDER HINGE
- 215.) RUDDER HINGE
- 216.) AILERON SEAL
- 217.) AILERON SEAL
- 218.) SPINNER
- 219.) FIRE INGRESS
- 220.) FIRE INGRESS
- 221.) AIR STARTER
- 222,) SLAT PULLY
- 223.) SLAT PULLY

XF-84H FUSELAGE STATIONS DIAGRAM

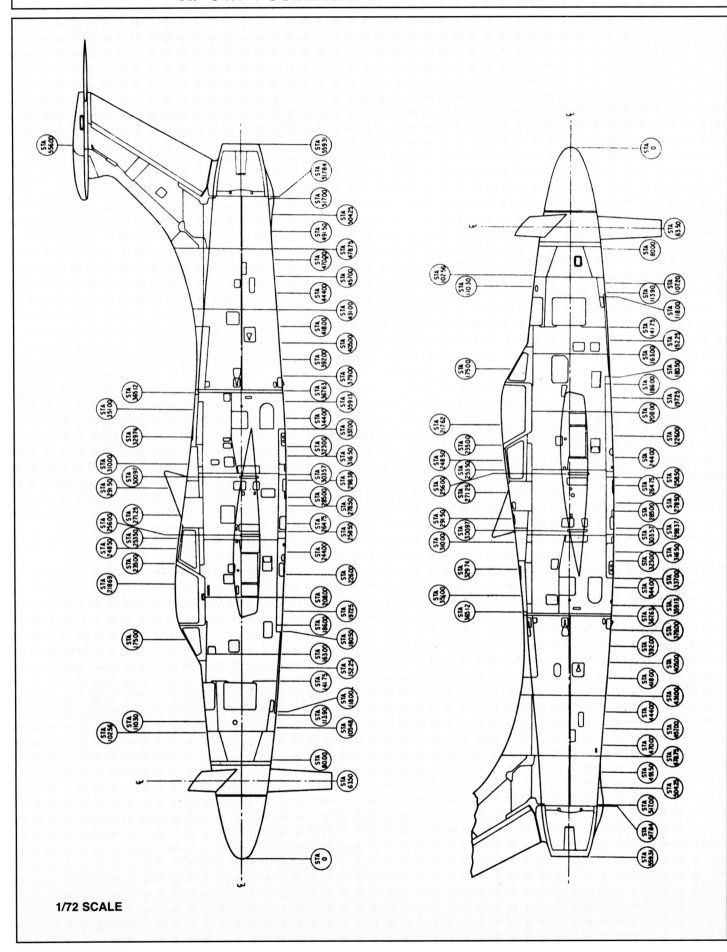

1/72 SCALE

AUXILIARY AIR INTAKES

XF-84H TAIL GROUP

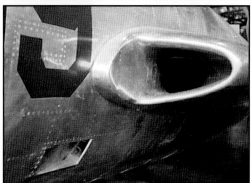
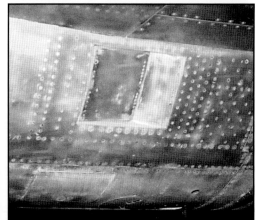
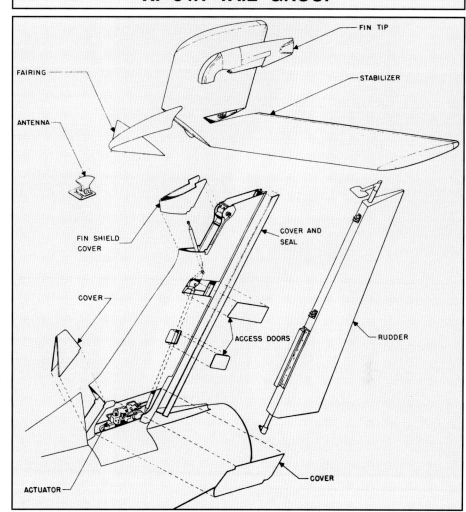

At top left, left forward fuselage flush air intake and louvre air intake just aft of nose gear door. Above left, right flush air intake with right flush air exit door beneath the wing. At left, left flush air exit door on lower fuselage beneath the wing. Bottom left, one of three NACA style after fuselage air intakes. Two were found on each side of the fuselage aft of the tail-to-fuselage joint. The 3rd was on the upper right side near the spine. Below, XF-84H tail group. (all Ginter)

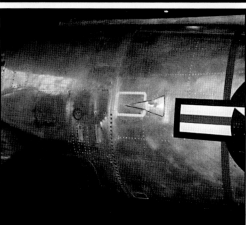

XF-84H MAIN LANDING GEAR

XF-84H MAIN LANDING GEAR WHEEL WELLS

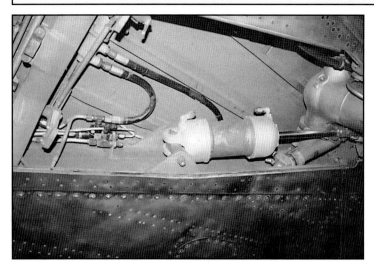

At top far left, left main landing gear looking outboard. (Ginter) At left, right main landing gear looking outboard. (Ginter) Bottom left, two views of the left main landing gear doors viewed from left front. (Ginter) At right, left main landing gear wheel well looking outboard. Note inner gear door (top of photo) closes after the gear is lowered and stays that way. Inner wheel well was painted with zinc chromate. (Ginter) Above, left main landing gear strut well looking aft. (Ginter) Bottom, left main landing gear wheel well looking inboard and aft. (Ginter)

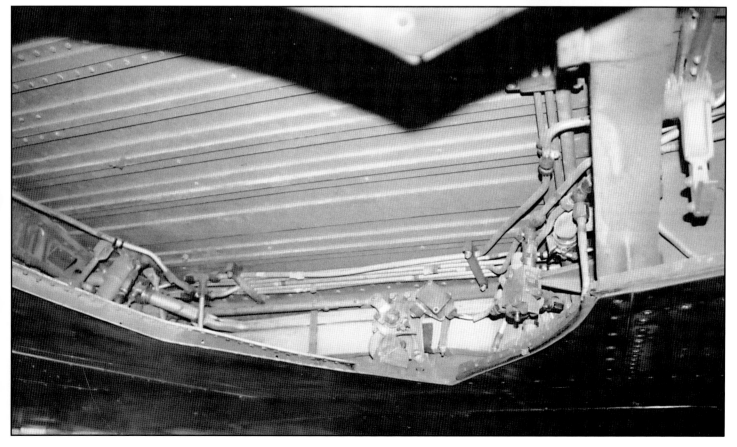

XF-84H NOSE LANDING GEAR

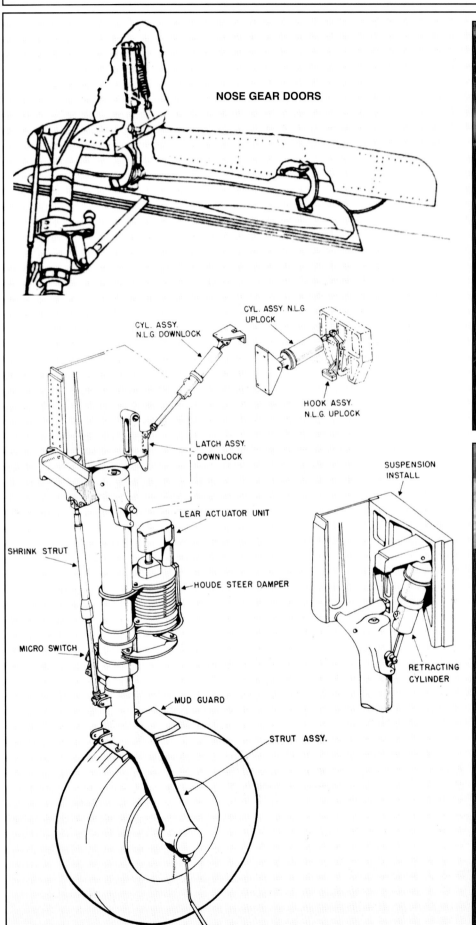

AEROPRODUCTS PROPELLER

The 12-foot supersonic hydraulic propeller employed on the XF-84H was manufactured by Aeroproducts. It was a constant speed, full-feathering and reversible unit. The blade model was D91A1-144. The light colored part of the hub rotated, the metal nose cone/spinner was stationary. By the way of the reduction gear, the propeller maintained a constant speed of 2,103rpm while the engine was turning 14,300rpm. (all photos Ginter)

ALLISON XT40-A-1 AFTERBURNING TURBOPROP INSTALLATION

The XT40-A-1 turboprop engine consisted of two gas turbine power sections connected by extension shafts to a single reduction gear box housing a single rotation propeller shaft and fitted with a Republic designed afterburner. The afterburner being a Navy requirement. Originally, it was to have driven two three-blade counter-rotating propellers like on the Douglas A2D-1 Skyshark, Convair R3Y-1/2 Tradewind, North American A2J-1 Super Savage, Lockheed XFV-1, and the Convair XFY-1 "Pogo". The original engine was tested with this configuration, but was changed to a short, single-rotation, three-blade Aeroproducts propeller before the airframes were constructed.

Each of the two power sections had eight combustion chambers of the through flow type and incorporated a 19-stage axial flow compressor directly coupled to a four-stage turbine. The power sections were secured to each other by brackets attached at the forward and aft ends of the compressor assemblies. The dual power unit also included the engine control system. Engine breathers were located on the top of each power section, and power section air bleeders and a de-icing air system were provided.

Accessories were mounted on the reduction gear box and the front end of each power section. The dual power unit was secured to the reduction gear assembly by the extension shafts.

The XT40-A-1 powerplant was of the continuous flow type. Air from the surrounding atmosphere was delivered through the ducts in each winglet and then into the compressor inlet housings of each power section. After the air was compressed, it flowed through diffusers which directed it to the eight cylindrical combustion chambers in each power section where fuel was introduced and the fuel-air mixture was burned. The resultant hot gases expanded through the multi-stage turbine, causing the turbine to rotate. The turbine in turn drives the compressor rotor, extension shafting, and the reduction gear box assembly. From the turbine, the gases traveled through an aperture formed by the inner exhaust cone and the turbine rear bearing support into the afterburner assembly. Thrust created by the gas discharge assisted in driving the aircraft forward.

The power section was supported at three points. Special mounts were installed on the outboard sides of each of the compressor sections, and a pedestal assembly with two rollers was attached to the power section forward tie bracket. The special mounts were clamped to the structure at station 365. The forward mount (pedestal assembly) rollers engaged the track installed on the underside of the fuselage at station 329. Shims were installed between the pedestal assembly and power section tie bracket. Access to the engine power sections was accomplished by removing the tail at the fuselage splice.

The power section accessory drive housings, mounted on the compressor section housing of each

Above, 3-bladed Aeroproducts prop tested on the T40-A-1. (AFFTC) Below, counter-rotating prop tested on the T40-A-1 on 24 September 1953. (Cradle of Aviation Museum)

power section, drove the fuel control and fuel pumps on the rear face of the compressor housing, the speed sensitive switch, and main oil pump and oil filter on the front part of the housing. Access to the accessories was through access door 65.

The reduction gear incorporated an independent dry sump oil system, two friction clutches, two safety coupling assemblies, thrustmeter, accessory drives, and the necessary gearing arrangement. The main reduction gear train consisted of one reduction stage with a reduction ratio of 6.8:1. This resulted in a propeller speed of 2,103rpm at 14,300 engine rpm.

The afterburner was located in the aft fuselage and consisted of two sections bolted together. The forward section was fitted into the intermediate pants duct connecting the engine to the afterburner at station 437. The injector assembly and spark plugs were in the forward section of the afterburner. The flame holder and tailpipe assemblies comprised the aft section. Access to the injector assembly, flame holder and tailpipe assemblies was accomplished by removing the bolts connecting the forward section of the afterburner to the aft.

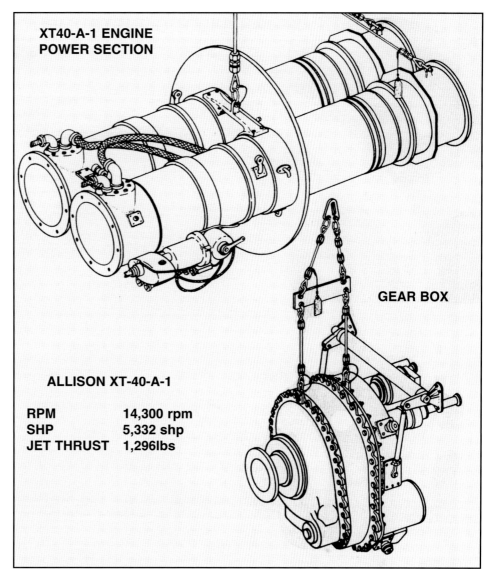

XT40-A-1 ENGINE POWER SECTION

GEAR BOX

ALLISON XT-40-A-1

RPM	14,300 rpm
SHP	5,332 shp
JET THRUST	1,296lbs

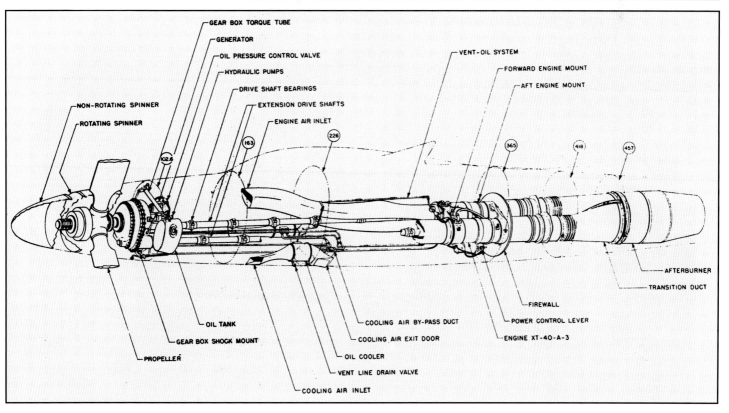

XF-84H PILOT'S INSTRUMENT PANEL

Geoff Hays

XF-84H PILOT'S LEFT - HAND CONSOLE

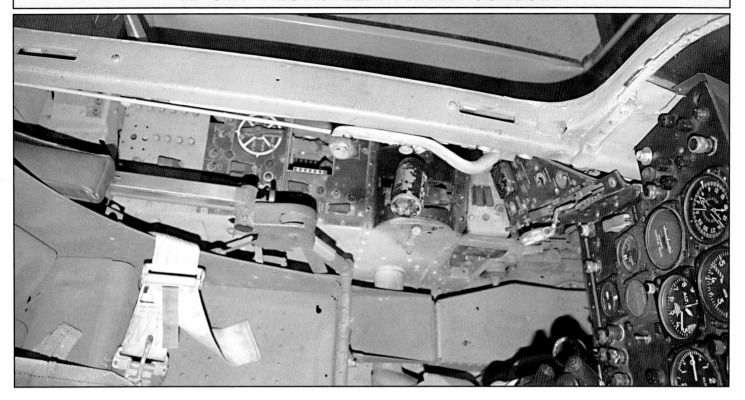

The cockpit except for black instrument panel, gages and stick grip was gray. The ejection seat was zinc chromate. (G. Hays)

XF-84H PILOT'S RIGHT - HAND CONSOLE

XF-84H PILOT'S EJECTION SEAT and STICK

XF-84H CANOPY AND VORTEX GATE

The upward and backward opening canopy on the XF-84H was the same as that used on the F-84F and RF-84F. Above, structure looking aft with canopy open. (Geoff Hays) Above right, armored windscreen. (Geoff Hays) At right, vortex gate just aft open canopy mechanism. (Geoff Hays) Below, two views of the open canopy. (AFFTC) Previous page, XF-84H ejection seat installation and canopy details. (Geoff Hays) Bottom left, pilot's stick and lower forward pilot's instrument panel. Cockpit except instrument panel was gray; seat was zinc chromate. (Geoff Hays)

XF-84H DEVELOPMENT AND TESTING

The XF-84H was designed by Alexander Kartveli and given Republic's designation AP-46. The two aircraft ultimately produced received serial numbers 51-17059 and 51-17060. The mock-up took form in an office building in downtown Manhattan as the experimental shop at Farmingdale was already in use with the prototype F-84F and the F-105 mock-up.

The first aircraft, s/n 51-17059, rolled out of Experimental Building 29N on 6 February 1954, and Republic scheduled preliminary ground runs for 8 March 1954. These were to occur in front of the Engineering Research Turboprop Engine Test Stand with the engine receiving fuel from a fuel line run from the test stand to the aircraft. In addition to normal test measurments, sound magnitudes and frequencies were measured at 24 various stations around the airplane during the run. These preliminary propeller-engine sound levels gave Republic a taste of what would be the aircraft's biggest issue, mind and body numbming sound vibrations for its ground crew, a trait which gave the aircraft its nickname, "Thunderscreech". Some gear box issues and a lot of hydraulic pump problems showed up in these initial tests.

Prior to these ground runs, the XT40-A-1 afterburner-propeller combination had to complete 50-hours of test stand qualification runs. The XF-84H's test objectives were to obtain basic data required to design and develop supersonic propellers and to obtain solutions to the problems involved in the use of high powered turboprop engines in fighter aircraft. The flight test data was necessary to validate previous static and wind tunnel test data.

On 20 April 1954, after the ground run tests had been completed, s/n 51-17059 posed for its public

---

Below, the number one XF-84H, S/N 51-17059, just before roll-out in Experimental Building 29N at Republic. Wings, landing gear and canopy area were esentially RF-84F components mated to a reworked fuselage and new T-tail. (Cradle of Aviation Museum)

relations debut with photos taken from every angle.

Above, the handsome 51-17059 on the taxiway at Republic on 6 February 1954. Ten F-84Fs and one RF-84F can be seen in the background. (Cradle of Aviation Museum)

XF-84H GROUND TEST SOUND LEVEL MEASURMENT STATIONS

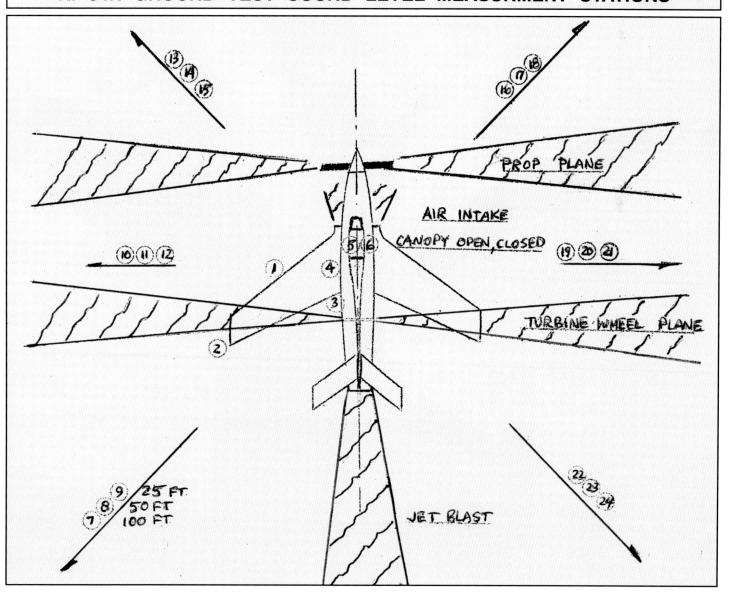

XF-84H S/N 51-17059 PUBLIC RELATIONS DEBUT, 20 APRIL 1954

XF-84H S/N 51-17059 PUBLIC RELATIONS DEBUT, 20 APRIL 1954

XF-84H S/N 51-17059 PUBLIC RELATIONS DEBUT, 20 APRIL 1954

At left, two views of the left fuselage side of S/N 51-17059 from above on 20 April 1954. (Fairchild Republic) At right, Republic test pilot Henry G. Beaird enters cockpit of F-84H, S/N 51-17059, on 20 April 1954 for the publicity photos. Beaird would make the first flight of this aircraft on 22 July 1955. (Cradle of Aviation Museum) Above, Beaird poses in the open cockpit of S/N 51-17059 on 20 April 1954 with new F-84Fs in the background. (Cradle of Aviation Museum) Bottom, view from 3/4 left rear on 20 April 1954 with canopy open. (Cradle of Aviation Museum)

The first aircraft, s/n 51-17059, did not arrive at the Air Force Flight Test Center (AFFTC), Edwards AFB, CA, until 4 December 1954 due to teething problems with the XT40-A-1 engine and its gear box. By 31 December, all major components had been assembled and the propeller and XT40-A-1 engine had been

XF-84H S/N 51-17059 FLIGHT TESTING AT EDWARDS AFB, CA

installed. For testing at Edwards, the Republic Project Engineer for the XF-84H was Joe Freeman and the Air Force Project Officer was MAJ Gordon O'Dell.

It was estimated that about a month would be needed to test the propeller/engine combination and for taxi tests to begin. However, taxi tests did not commence until 28 March 1955. Difficulty was encountered immediately on the loss of oil pressure to the XT40-A-1 power sections upon acceleration or deceleration of the airplane.

Republic Aircraft Company concentrated on a solution to this problem for the following two months before a satisfactory oil system configuration was determined. The changes made in the system included larger diameter oil lines, relocation of the forward bleed valve, the use of a barometric valve as the oil tank pressurizing agent and the inclusion of a manual shutoff valve in each of the engine compartment bleed lines.

Taxi runs were made up to IAS of 160 knots, with the airplane lifting off at that speed. A left wing rolloff was experienced upon liftoff. In general, directional control using rudder was considered to be marginal when the throttle was retarded to the flight idle position at 100 knots and would result in loss of directional control using rudder control only. However, use of brakes provided adequate control.

The preliminary afterburner test stand runs were started in May 1955. Propeller surging was encountered on these runs as well as failure of the air-turbine fuel pump bearings and erratic afterburner fuel scheduling. The Aeroproducts flight propeller was installed in June 1955 and ground tests to simulate flight conditions were started. Propeller surge developed on these simulated flights, too, which made it impossible to continue with the tests until Aeroproducts reworked the propeller hub.

It was during this time that Republic found out how literally nauseating the noise and vibration of the supersonic propeller was to the ground crew when running the engine on the ground. The outer 12-to-18 inches of the propeller were supersonic at all times which banned the aircraft from ground run-ups on main base and from taxiing near the tower or hangars. When flight tests com-

---

Below, public unveiling of the XF-84H at Edwards AFB, CA, in January 1955. (USAF)

menced, the Thunderscreech would be towed to the runway about a mile from the tower and even then blankets were put over the radio shelf in the tower to protect them, and the tower crew would put on ear protection until take-off was complete.

The program was banished to North Base, just below Rocket Hill. The noise level, which was well within the pain level, was so loud that it was heard as far as twenty miles away. The debilitating effects were most severe when standing just off the plane of the prop. The safest position was in front or behind the aircraft.

On 21 July 1955, Republic test pilot Henry G. Beaird made the first flight at 06:27 local time. The flight objectives were for operational and safety checks as well as power plant and airplane preliminary control evaluation. After the first flight, Henry Beaird had described the aircraft as

Above and below, ground runs and system testing were completed at North Base prior to the first flight of 51-17059. (AFFTC)

"a real honey", saying "it had speed and maneuverability and exhibited good take-off characteristics and excellent flight performance."

The take-off gross weight was 22,970lbs with center-of-gravity (CG) at 14.1% MAC with the wheels down and the takeoff fin (Vortex Gate) locked at zero degrees. The emergency hydraulic fan (RAT) was extended as was the leading edge slats. The flaps were set at 20°. Barometric pressure was 27.57 inch Hg., free air temperature was 73°F., wind was south at 5-knots, take-off direction was 40°, specific gravity of the fuel was .695 and the fuel temperature was 83°F. All controls checked out normally prior to take-off; propeller indicated a blade angle of 18° and turbine vibration was below 1.5 mils on the ground.

The nose wheel lifted off at 90 knots and the airplane was airborne at 160-165 knots after a roll of approximately 7,650 feet. Some lateral instability was shown following take-off but was a result of overcontrol rather than aerodynamic issues. The leading edge slats closed at 180 knots and the gear was retracted. A power lever angle of 90° was held in the climb to 6,000 feet. Climb speed was approximately 200 knots to the test altitude of 20,000 ft. Power was reduced to 80° power lever angle in the climb from 6,000 to 20,000 feet. During the climb, an occasional intermittent random bunting of the power plant and propeller was observed in the amount of 100rpm peak-to-peak variation and was associated with high power settings.

The left power section oil pressure fluctuated during left turns, slight nose overs, and to deceleration caused by extended gear, flaps, or slats. The oil pressure returned to normal after completion of these maneuvers. Power-off stalls were performed at 20,000 feet with the flaps at 20° and the gear and slats extended. Aileron buffet was experienced at 150 knots and the nose dropped through at 130 knots. Adverse roll off, yaw or other control issues were not present in the stalls. A power-on stall at 70° power lever angle was made in the same configuration with aileron buffet noticed at 145 knots. Some moderate dynamic

Above, Republic's test pilot Henry Beaird climbs for altitude during the XF-84H's 1st flight on 21 July 1955. Beaird described the plane as "a real honey" after he landed. (Republic) Below and bottom of next page, the number one aircraft, S/N 51-17059, sits on the lake bed after a test flight. Note the deployed RAT at the base of the vertical fin, extended slats and the open speed brakes. (AFFTCHO)

longitudinal and directional stability was performed with more than adequate damping demonstrated. Considerable positive dihedral effect was demonstrated to the highest speed tested, 260 knots indicated airspeed (IAS) in the climb.

Loss of emergency hydraulic pressure was noted after 26 minutes of flight, whereupon the flight was terminated. Lateral control remained sensitive during the flight and appeared to be improved following loss of the emergency system and during landing. This may have been attributed to aerodynamic requirements, pilot familiarization, or some hydraulic characteristic associated with the loss of the emergency system.

Ground examination showed the emergency pump delivery pressure line had failed. The let-down for landing was made at approximately 190-200 knots. The approach was made at 170 knots with 60-80° power lever angle carried over the fence and with flight idle power carried at the touch-

At right, actress Joy Lansing posing with XF-84H, S/N 51-17059, at Bakersfield, CA, after its retirement in 1958. (AFFTCHO)

down speed of about 150 knots. Beaird had pulled the power lever into the ground idle regime but apparently the Beta control was inoperative as a 20° blade angle position was shown. This caused considerable braking to be used to stop and to taxi the aircraft. As a result, both brakes caught fire upon shut down after taxiing back to the ramp.

This type of landing became the norm with eleven out of twelve test flights ending with a precautionary emergency landing due to some kind of system problem. When the XF-84H program was drawn up, it was estimated that the flight test program would require 140 flight hours. But in reality, it only lasted less than 10 hours.

On subsequent ground runs and test flights, nose wheel shimmy became a problem and was finally reduced to acceptable levels with much tinkering. In August 1955, the nose gear collapsed while the aircraft was being towed to the hangar, allow-

Above and below, the 2nd XF-84H, S/N 51-17060, on roll-out at Farmingdale on 28 January 1955. (Cradle of Aviation Museum)

XF-84H S/N 51-17060 FLIGHT TESTING AT EDWARDS AFB, CA

ing the propeller to strike the ground. Another test flight in December was aborted because of only the partial retraction of the nose gear. The gear indicator had indicated unsafe until after touchdown, but indicated safe during landing roll. Several of the nose gear's hydraulic components had to be replaced before testing could continue. It must be remembered that the nose gear was an off-the-shelf RF-84F unit designed for a much lighter aircraft than the XF-84H.

Although the XF-84H had good flight characteristics including a high rate of roll and low speed handling, it did have a number of weaknesses that could have been easily fixed if a production contract had been issued. Because of the high torque of the XT40, substantial right rudder deflection (35°) and trim (20°) was built into the design. However, the left rudder deflection (15°) and trim (6°) was insufficient at low approach speeds. The extreme forward CG on the XF-84H proved to be a blessing and a curse. Because of the CG, the aircraft had no pitch-up tendencies at high

Above and below, two views of 51-17060 at the 1956 open house at Edwards AFB. Red intake lips were added along with a red stripe on the inboard side of the wing flap. (Ginter collection and Wayne Morris)

angles of attack and high G-forces. It took off rapidly with very little aft stick. The forward CG gave the "H" good stall characteristics with no tendencies to roll in power-off stalls. In power-on stalls a slight roll was expe-

rienced due to the torque of the prop. The curse only created a minor issue in that it caused a somewhat high approach speed of 130 knots in order not to run out of elevator power.

Although Republic had estimated the XF-84H's maximum speed at 680mph it never exceeded 450mph due to the high levels of driveshaft vibration above 400 knots and the tendency to porpoise and roll at those speeds caused by the propeller governor surging. These issues could cause violent roll as the entire airframe tried to rotate around the propshaft.

The second XF-84H, s/n 51-17060, was rolled out at Farmingdale, NJ, on 28 January 1955. After initial testing at Republic it was delivered by means of a C-124 to Edwards AFB, CA, on 14 May 1955. Only twelve flights were made in both aircraft before the project was cancelled. Eight were flown in 51-17059 and four in 51-17060. All but one flight was made by Beaird. The last flight was made on 9 October 1956 in s/n 51-17060 with Republic's Lin Hendrix at the controls. Hendrix summed up his

Above, Hank Beaird (note Confederate flag in the canopy window) in the second XF-84H, S/N 51-17060, over the Mojave in late 1955. The black paint found on the spine of 059 was not found on 060. (AFFTCHO) Below, S/N 51-17060, being towed past the tower at Edwards after a test flight. (Ginter collection)

feelings in the August 1977 issue of Aeroplane Monthly. After landing, he told Republic's chief engineer, Joe Freeman, "You aren't big enough and

there aren't enough of you engineers to get in that thing again". Freeman stood 6' 4" tall and weighed in at 235lbs. Although both aircraft had an afterburner, it was never used in flight.

After the program was terminated, the two aircraft languished at Edwards until 51-17059 was donated to the Kern County Historical Society and put on display at Meadows Field in Bakersfield, CA. in 1958. 51-17060 did not survive; it was scrapped at Edwards. 059 was then put on a pedestal in front of the airport terminal building where it was dedicated on 27 April 1958. In 1992, the US Air Force Museum took the aircraft off its pole and took it back to Ohio where it now resides in the experimental aircraft hangar along with the Republic XF-91 and a Republic FICON fighter.

Above, 51-17059 during new airport terminal construction in 1958. (Harry Gann) Below, aircraft in the 1970s. (Ginter) Bottom, 059 on its pole in 1959. (Ginter col.)

McDONNELL XF-88B SUPERSONIC PROPELLER TEST BED

At top, the XF-88B takes off from the McDonnell St. Louis plant for its maiden flight on 14 March 1943 with its first test prop, a 4-blade unit. Because the turbojet was seperate from the prop-jet on the XF-88B, the aircraft could take off without the supersonic propeller's ill effects on the ground crew, airport, and nearby community. (McDonnell) Above, short 3-blade supersonic prop with spherical spinner being tested at NACA Langley. (NACA via Rick Koehnen) Below, short 3-blade supersonic prop with aerodynamic spinner at NACA Langley. (NACA via Robert F. Dorr) Bottom, long 3-blade Aeroproducts supersonic propeller as flown on the XF-84H fitted on the XF-88B at NACA Langley. Note yellow NACA emblem on the tail. (NACA via Rick Koehnen)

The McDonnell XF-88 "Voodoo" (see Air Force Legends #205) was one of the competitors in the penetration fighter program. Of the eight submissions, only McDonnell and Lockheed (XF-90) received contracts for two aircraft each. First flown on 20 October 1948, it had finished its flight test program and been put in storage at McDonnell by the time Republic received its contract for the XF-84H. The XF-84H was originally scheduled to begin its flight test program starting with taxi tests at Edwards AFB in the spring of 1953. However, due to the long gestation period caused by the engines, afterburners and gear boxes related to the XT40-A-1, that did not happen until two years later, in the spring of 1955.

The number two XF-88 was pulled from storage and modified to become the back-up supersonic propeller test bed to the XF-84H. Designated the XF-88B, the conversion was straightforward as the aircraft retained its afterburning J34s and added a single, much simpler Allison XT38-A-5 2,650 eshp turboprop engine. The less powerful arrangement did not require the two extremely long propshafts, only one short one, and a less complex gear box. The arrangement also gave the option of only having to use the turboprop when wanted or needed instead of it being on 100% of the time when the engine was running like on the XF-84H. This eliminated the severe noise problems and damage to the ground crew,s senses.

The XF-88B made its first flight on 14 March 1953 and began a testing program with NACA that lasted until January 1958. Because the XF-88B flew two years before the XF-84H and was more user friendly, it was able to test the various supersonic props originally slated for the "Thunderscreech". The propellers were produced by Curtiss, Hamilton Standard, and Aeroproducts. Unlike the XF-84H, the XF-88B did go supersonic. The highest speed attained was 1.12 Mach in a power-dive while powered by the turboprop only.

MAINTRACK, PROJECT-X 1/72 VACUFORM XF-84H KIT PX-030

Maintrack's Project-X kit number PX-030 came with 28 white vacuform parts, 3 clear vacuform parts, 11 white metal pieces and a decal sheet with decals for both XF-84Hs, S/Nos 51-17059 and 51-17060.

The most difficult part of this build was the goofy way the props and spinner were constructed. This kit utilized an inner and outer two-part spinner fitted over a fuselage plug. It was hard to build and was very fragile. The prop blades were offered as vacuform parts or as white metal units. To speed up construction, the Airfix F-84F kit was raided for cockpit and landing gear parts.

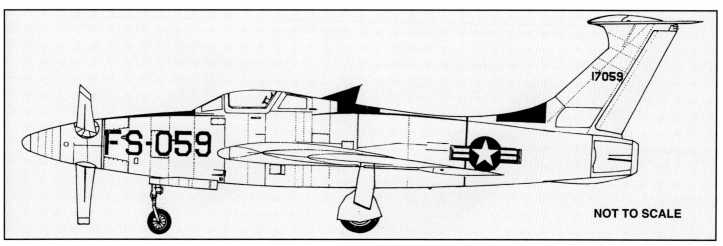

NOT TO SCALE

1/72 RESIN ANIGRAND XF-84H KIT AA-2059

The Anigrand 1/72 scale kit comes with decals for 51-17059, 21 resin parts and a clear plastic canopy. Fit is excellent with almost no filler needed. Construction is so easy that if it wasn't for the drying time of the paint you could finish it on a Saturday afternoon. Minor negative points are the heavy panel lines, absence of the NACA auxilary intake on the spine and a cloudy canopy. My kit was also missing the control stick.

1/48 RESIN COLLECT AIRE XF-84H KIT 4835

The Collect-Aire kit offered a resin kit with plastic and metal detail parts and decals. We were unable to find a used kit or a built up example to share with you. One kit was recently on E-Bay and sold for almost $300.00.

EXECUFORM 1/72 VACUFORM XF-84H KIT

The 1996 Execuform kit by Mike Herrill was comprised of 11 white vacuform parts and 1 clear vacuform canopy. It also included a resin prop spinner and 10 white metal pieces including the prop blades. No decals were provided. The plastic was glossy smoth without and panel lines. Due to time constraints only the wing and horizontal stabilizer received any scribing. The kit was supplied by Louis Santos.

6.) Anti-torque fin.
7.) NACA flush air inlet.
8.) Debris deflector.
9.) Flush air inlet.
10.) Flush air exit doors.
11.) Fuselage tailcone joint.
12.) Speed brakes.

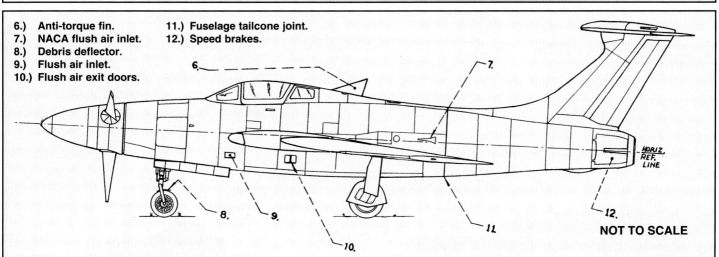

NOT TO SCALE

EXECUFORM 1/72 VACUFORM XF-84H KIT

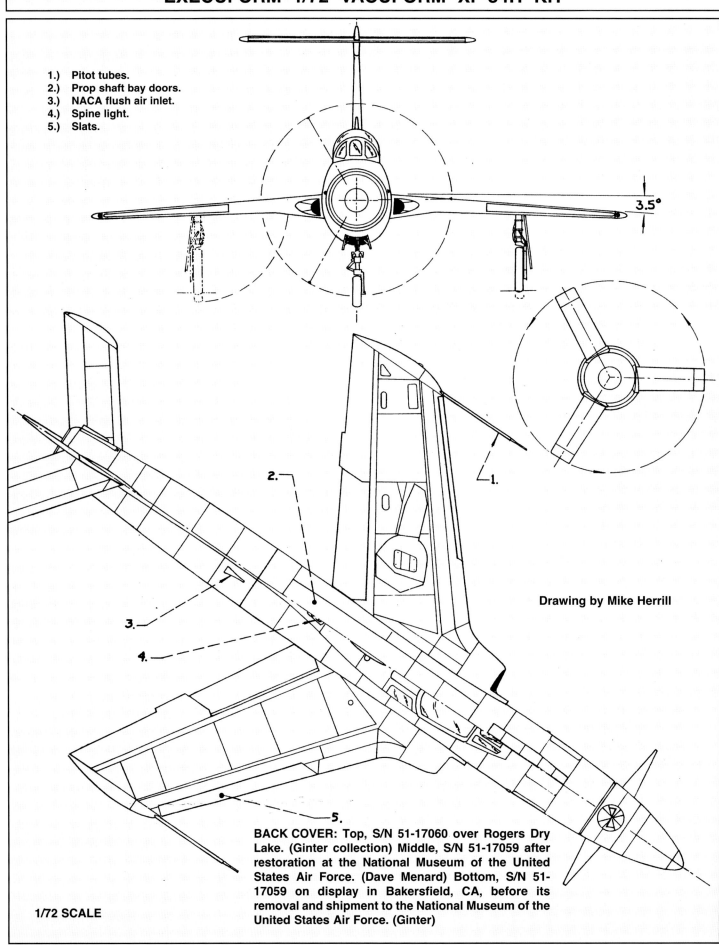

1.) Pitot tubes.
2.) Prop shaft bay doors.
3.) NACA flush air inlet.
4.) Spine light.
5.) Slats.

Drawing by Mike Herrill

BACK COVER: Top, S/N 51-17060 over Rogers Dry Lake. (Ginter collection) Middle, S/N 51-17059 after restoration at the National Museum of the United States Air Force. (Dave Menard) Bottom, S/N 51-17059 on display in Bakersfield, CA, before its removal and shipment to the National Museum of the United States Air Force. (Ginter)

1/72 SCALE